To Whom Did Jacob Preach?

Analecta Gorgiana

1047

Series Editor

George Anton Kiraz

Analecta Gorgiana is a collection of long essays and short monographs which are consistently cited by modern scholars but previously difficult to find because of their original appearance in obscure publications. Carefully selected by a team of scholars based on their relevance to modern scholarship, these essays can now be fully utilized by scholars and proudly owned by libraries.

To Whom Did Jacob Preach?

Susan Ashbrook Harvey

gorgias press

2011

Gorgias Press LLC, 954 River Road, Piscataway, NJ, 08854, USA

www.gorgiaspress.com

Copyright © 2011 by Gorgias Press LLC

Originally published in 2010

2011 ܟܕ

ISBN 978-1-4632-0095-4   ISSN 1935-6854

Reprinted from the 2010 Piscataway edition.

Printed in the United States of America

TO WHOM DID JACOB PREACH?

SUSAN ASHBROOK HARVEY

Jacob of Serugh is known especially through the huge corpus of his mimre (verse homilies), several hundred of which survive to us.[1] Preached over a career of some decades amongst villages, towns, and monasteries in the district of Serugh, to the southwest of Edessa, these homilies cover a wide array of topics, biblical, monastic, theological, liturgical. Scholars have generally focused on these homilies as the work of a master poet and theologian. They have analyzed Jacob's poetic craft, his theological acumen, and his

---

[1] See the index of first lines in *Homilies of Mar Jacob of Serugh / Homiliae selectae Mar-Jacobi Serughensis*, Paris/Leipzig, [1]1905; Piscataway, NJ: Gorgias Press, [2]2006 (ed. S.P. Brock), vol. 6, 372–99.

In this article, I use the following abbreviations:

Bedjan = *Homilies of Mar Jacob of Serugh / Homiliae selectae Mar-Jacobi Serughensis*, Paris/Leipzig, [1]1905; Piscataway, NJ: Gorgias Press, [2]2006 (ed. S.P. Brock), 6 vols.

DR = *Downside Review*

FH = *Jacob of Serugh, Select Festal Homilies*, intro. and trans. Thomas Kollamparampil, Rome: Centre for Indian and Inter-religious Studies, 1997.

HTM = Holy Transfiguration Monastery

MFC = Message of the Fathers of the Church

OCA = Orientalia Christiana Analecta

PO = *Patrologia Orientalis*

SVTQ = *St. Vladimir's Theological Quarterly*.

I have occasionally altered the older translations used here, for clearer sense.

articulation of the varied strains of Syriac biblical, doctrinal, and liturgical traditions woven into the tapestry of his teachings.[2]

But what do we know about the congregations who heard these sermons? Sometimes the content of Jacob's homilies indicates a monastic audience; sometimes Jacob is clearly addressing an urban church, or perhaps the smaller civic setting of the scattered villages and towns that dotted the landscape of his region. At times, he preaches in terms that seem inclusive of both the monastic and the civic lives, as if trying to present a sermon that would speak to both locations, with their differing daily lives and demands. Most often, it is impossible to know where, or when, or to whom he was preaching. Many of his biblical sermons, for example, seem addressed to any and every Christian, no matter their profession, vocation, age, gender, or social status. It is precisely this timeless—or even, generic—quality that caused Jacob's homilies to be cherished and chanted over many centuries, recited in vigil services or daily offices with little concern for their relevance to any immediate context.[3] Like the Bible itself, Jacob's homilies could stand outside of time in the wisdom they offered. This same timelessness is often frustrating for historians, however,

---

[2] For example, Alwan, Khalil. *Anthropologie de Jacques de Saroug: l'homme 'microcosme', avec une bibliographie générale raisonnée*, Jounieh, Liban: Imprimerie Moderne "Kreim" / Rome: Pontificium Institutum Orientalium Studiorum, 1988; Bou Mansour, P. Tanios. *La théologie de Jacques de Saroug*, Kaslik: Université Saint Esprit, 1993; Golitzin, Alexander. "The Image and Glory of God in Jacob of Serugh's Homily 'On that Chariot that Ezekel the Prophet saw'," *SVTQ* 47:3/4 (2003): 323–64; Papoutsakis, Manolis. "Formulaic Language in the Metrical Homilies of Jacob of Serugh," in Lavenant, René, ed. *Symposium Syriacum VII*, 445–51, OCA, 256, Rome: Pontificium Institutum Orientalium Studiorum, 1998; Harvey, S.A. "Bride of Blood, Bride of Light: Biblical Women as Images of Church in Jacob of Serugh," in Kiraz, George, ed. *Malphono w-Rabo d-Malphone: Festschrift for Sebastian P. Brock*, 189–218, Piscataway, NJ: Gorgias Press, 2008.

[3] Barsoum, Patriarch Ignatius Aphram I. *The Scattered Pearls: A History of Syriac Literature and Sciences*, trans. and ed. Matti Moosa, 2nd rev. ed., 77, 92, Piscataway, NJ: Gorgias press, 2003.

who must strain to find any hint of historical setting, place, or event; any reference to the turbulence and tumult indelibly woven into the times in which Jacob lived.

But Jacob did preach, to real people in real lives, in real places. Jacob's audience was important, for without them these homilies would not have been written or delivered. How might the various congregations to whom Jacob preached be visible to us? Who were they? How did they affect his homilies? How were they present in his preaching?[4] And why should they matter to us now, so many centuries later, in our continuing appreciation for Jacob's work? The answers to these questions may help us consider anew the legacy of Jacob's homiletic wealth.

1. THE CHURCH IN THE WORLD

Jacob of Serugh chanted his homilies during the late fifth and early sixth centuries, in the easternmost part of the Roman Empire. It was "the best of times, and the worst of times" for Christians in this region.[5] Christianity reigned triumphant as the state religion of the Roman Empire; liturgically and institutionally, the church was blossoming into its full glory. Monastic life was well-established, the canonical ranks of the clergy clarified, and the integration of church life with family and civic duties everywhere apparent. For Jacob, the fullness of God's creation was only now apparent, with the ascendancy of Christianity over the other religions of the Empire's realm:

---

[4] Important discussion of related evidence for late antique congregations is well treated in Cunningham, Mary B., and Pauline Allen. *Preacher and Audience: Studies in Early Christian and Byzantine Homiletics*, Leiden: Brill 1998, esp. Mayer, Wendy. "John Chrysostom: Extraordinary Preacher, Ordinary Audience," 105–38; Maxwell, Jaclyn. *Christianization and Communication in Late Antiquity: John Chrysostom and his Congregation in Antioch*, Cambridge: Cambridge University Press, 2006; Taft, Robert. *Through Their Own Eyes: Liturgy as the Byzantines Saw It*, Berkeley, CA; InterOrthodox Press, 2006.

[5] Cf. the opening line of Charles Dickens' *A Tale of Two Cities*.

The diligent Son of God uprooted and cast down the temples
    of the demons,
and lo, He planted churches at the ends of all the world.

...

He built up creation with gold and precious stones,
and brought forth hymns of praise from desolate lands.
He made the world into a king's palace full of lovely things,
and set the Cross therein like a pearl column.
He burned incense to sweeten the earth with a sweet fragrance
From a root that Virgin Soil gave the world.

...

The air that was troubled by the fumes of sacrificial victims,
which ascended through it to polluted demons, is become clear
    and pure and sweet.[6]

Jacob could sing the glories of triumph with grand majesty.
But what did the life of the church mean for people now, amidst
Christian dominance? Alas, Jacob's homilies are replete with the
hazards of complacency. In the civic community, whether of village
or city, Jacob encountered Christian devotion in competition with
the demands of worldly life much more than with other religions.
Work, business, family, household: all required much attention, all
demanded great energy. Religious devotion was one more demand.
The church now offered long and elaborate liturgies, in addition to
daily services morning and night, as well as celebrations for the
great feasts of the church: the feasts of the life of Christ
(Annunciation, Nativity, Baptism, Presentation in the Temple),
Lent, Palm Sunday and Passion Week, Easter, Ascension and
Pentecost; as well as commemorations of the saints, including the
Virgin Mary, whose Dormition was just coming to be celebrated.[7]
Justly did Jacob exhort,

----

[6] "On the Parable of the Leaven, by Mar Jacob, Bishop of Serugh",
trans. HTM [Dana Miller], *The True Vine* 3 (1989): 45–57, at 47, ll. 28–42.

[7] For the development of the Syriac liturgy and the daily offices in the
context of eastern Christianity see, e.g., Mateos, Juan. *Lelya-Sapra: Essai
d'interprétation des matines chaldeennes*, OCA, 156, Rome: Pontificium
Institutum Orientalium Studiorum, 1959; idem, *La célébration de la parole*

The Church in the world is a great harbour, full of peace; whoever toils, let him come in and rest at her table. Her doors are open, and her eye is good and her heart is wide. Her table is full, and sweet is her mingled (cup) to them that are worthy. You lovers of the world, come in from wandering in the evil world, and rest in the inn that is full of comfort to him that enters it.[8]

But who had the time? Jacob laments at length on the liturgical laxity of civic life. People were too busy to come! Distracted by their business affairs, their work, the marketplace and its fashions, people passed the church by. Or, they came to liturgy and fidgeted. As the liturgy proceeded in its stately unfolding, they stood impatiently with their thoughts elsewhere. "Do not let your mind remain in the market at your business," Jacob pleaded in one homily,

Why is your thought gone forth and distracted after affairs, so that when you are here [in church] you are not here, but there? Out amid the markets your mind is wandering, (taken up) with reckonings and profits; go fetch it…Stand not with one half of you within and one half without, lest when you are divided

---

dans la liturgie Byzantine, OCA, 191, Rome, Pontificium Institutum Orientalium Studiorum, 1971; Bradshaw, Paul. Daily Prayer in the Early Church, 72–110, Oxford: Oxford University Press, 1982; Taft, Robert. The Liturgy of the Hours in East and West: the Origins of the Divine Office and its Meaning for Today, esp. 225–48, Collegeville, Minn: Liturgical Press, 1986; Talley, Thomas. The Origins of the Liturgical Year, New York: Pueblo Publishing Co., 1986. Useful bibliography in general may be found in Jones, C., G. Wainwright, E.J. Yarnold and P. Bradshaw. The Study of Liturgy, rev. ed. New York: Oxford University Press / London: SPCK, 1992, esp. Cobb, P. "The Liturgy of the Word in the Early Church", pp. 219–29, and Yarnold, E.J. "The Liturgy of the Faithful in the Fourth and Early Fifth Century", pp. 230–44.

[8] "A Homily of Mar Jacob of Serugh On the Reception of the Holy Mysteries," trans. Hugh Connolly, DR 27 (1908): 278–87, at 279.

your prayer lose itself between the two parts. Stand at prayer a
united and complete and true [person].[9]

In his homily "On the Reception of the Mysteries", Jacob
described and explained the liturgy in its elaborate parts. First there
was the liturgy of the Word, with its invocational prayers, psalms,
hymns, biblical readings from prophets, apostles, and gospels; the
homily to explicate the scriptures; and the departure of the
catechumens. Then began the Liturgy of the Faithful, with its
litanies, the Lord's Prayer, the consecration, epiclesis, anaphora, the
giving and receiving of the Eucharist amidst prayers whispered by
the faithful, intoned by priest and deacons, and sung by the choirs
to finish at last in the prayers of dismissal. In providing this scenic
tour through the divine liturgy, Jacob's concern was not that people
did not appreciate the beauty this ritual mosaic comprised
(although that did dismay him). Rather, he was appalled because
people were leaving early—with the dismissal of the catechumens,
half-way through the service! without receiving communion!—so
as to go to the marketplace. Or, they took the excuse of the church
doors opening for the catechumens to leave in order to arrive late
and sneak inside—in time for communion, but having missed the
entire Liturgy of the Word, because they had been at other
business. Interestingly, it was not the harried housewife that
worried him, but the businessman who was hard at work making
money and increasing his wealth, rather than attending to the
health of his soul (and body—for Jacob waxed lyrical on the
nourishment for health that peaceful time within the liturgy could
provide).[10]

People came late to liturgy; people left early. They were
restless in their places. During long sermons, they grew visibly
impatient. Jacob's poetry could be admonitory: "Rebellious
children, do not grow weary with lengthy [sermons]... Do not
grow bored... pay attention to me, that I may address you

---

[9] "A Homily of Mar Jacob of Serugh On the Reception," 279.

[10] For examples of similar behaviors in other late antique
congregations, see Sheerin, Daniel. *The Eucharist*, esp. 236–392, MFC, 7,
Wilmington, Del: Michael Glazier, 1986. On wild behavior: pp. 319–48.

pleasantly." Preaching a homily on the life of St. Ephrem that had clearly gone on too long for some people's tastes, Jacob upbraided his congregation:

> Chosen Ephrem did not grow bored when he taught;
> you should not be bored when you hear the story about him.
> He struggled patiently against heresies;
> therefore, you should patiently follow the discourse about him.
>
> …
>
> Pay uninterrupted attention to me as I speak at length
> of the athlete who diligently carried on the struggle.[11]

Jacob fretted not only about the impatience of his parishioners, but also about their carelessness. For the memorial services for the dead, people were to bring bread and wine for the priest to offer in commemoration of their beloved departed and their families. Instead, they sent their offerings with their servants, rather than coming in person. Even the women, Jacob complained, seemed more inclined to mourn the dead in the cemeteries where they could weep unimpeded, than to attend the memorials on their behalf. Families "forgot" about the portion of inheritance the dead had bequeathed for such memorial services, instead dividing the money for their own purposes. A cavalier attitude prevailed. "Good customs are not practiced as they ought;/ but lo, the world is diligently careful over vanities….Such things as be needful are not performed wisely,/ and those that ought not, are done unjustly."[12] How luminous the beauty, then, of the faithful parishioner.

---

[11] "A Metrical Homily on Holy Mar Ephrem by Mar Jacob of Serugh", ed. and trans. Joseph P. Amar, *PO* 47 (1995): 1–76, at pp. 57, 63, 67, vv. 128, 145–7, 169. Ephrem the Syrian was clearly worried about sleepy parishioners during the night vigil on the eve of the Nativity feast. See Ephrem, *Hymns on Nativity* 1: 72, 77–81; 4: 51–2; 5: 6–7, 9; 21:2, 10. These are translated in McVey, Kathleen. *Ephrem the Syrian: Hymns*, 61–217, New York: Paulist Press, 1989.

[12] "On the Reposed, by Mar Jacob, Bishop of Serugh," trans. HTM [Dana Miller], *The True Vine* 5 (1990): 41–53, at p. 46, ll. 121–6; also trans. Hugh Connolly, *DR* 29 (1910): 260–70.

> Blessed is the widow that bears her sacrifice [of bread] in her
>   own hands,
> and the bereaved that carries it and glories in it.
>   …
> Like a priest, she brings her vow into the Lord
> as with pain she commemorates her dead over her oblation.
>   …
> The prosphora is in her hands, tears are in her eyes, and praise
>   in her mouth,
> And the excellency of her faith, like her oblation, is great.[13]

Elsewhere, one hears a certain weariness in Jacob's voice when he spoke on fasting in Lent: "It is good to speak about fasting if there is a desire for fasting in the ears of the hearers, so that what is said with knowledge may be received with love…It is much more important and excellent that one should fast rather than to speak about fasting."[14]

Even if one fended off the cares of the business world or the stresses of the marketplace, then the city offered other insidious distractions in the form of the theater. In this regard, Jacob joins a huge chorus of late antique homilists who railed against the spectacles performed in the popular arenas, the entertainments by which the quality of civic life was often measured in the ancient Mediterranean.[15] Jacob's list of the theater's dangers is standard

---

[13] "On the Reposed", at p. 53, ll. 283–94.

[14] FH 9 (On the 40 Days' Fasting), p. 234, v. 1.

[15] Relevant here are Maxwell, *Christianization and Communication*, 51–60, 133–6; and Leyerle, Blake. *Theatrical Shows and Ascetic Lives: John Chrysostom's Attack on Spiritual Marriage*, 13–74, Berkeley: University of California Press, 2001. For the significance of the larger culture, see Potter, D.S., and D.J. Mattingly. *Life, Death and Entertainment in the Roman Empire*, Ann Arbor: University of Michigan Press, 1999, esp. ch. 6, Dodge, Hazel. "Amusing the Masses: Buildings for Entertainment and Leisure in the Roman World," pp. 205–55, 336–8; and ch. 7, Potter, David S. "Entertainers in the Roman Empire," 256–325, 338–41. For the material evidence for the theater and its civic significance in late antique Syria, see Butcher, Kevin. *Roman Syria and the Near East*, 223–69, Los Angeles: Getty Publications / London: British Museum Press, 2003; and Ball, Warwick.

fare for the time: the lascivious appearance of the performers, seductive music, exotic dancing, heady perfumes and incense; comedies and tragedies based on traditional ("pagan") mythology that churned the emotions, riled one's behavior, and infected the mind with stories of gods and goddesses, sex, violence, greed, and horror. As Jacob complained, people were dismissive of his criticisms (—and with the same defense of television and movies often heard today!). He mimicked their self-justifications:

> It is a game (i.e., a spectacle), they say, not [religion]. What will you lose if I laugh?...The dancing gladdens me, and, while I confess God, I also take pleasure in the play...I am a baptized (Christian) even as you are, and I confess one Lord... I do not go that I may believe, but I go that I may laugh.[16]

Against such competition, one can see that the pressure for good preaching, with rousing, vibrant stories of thrilling adventures and exotic deeds could have been very strong, indeed. (And one can see why, in his sermons on biblical stories, Jacob struggled mightily to explain exactly how to understand in the right way, the sex, violence, greed and horror of many biblical episodes.[17])

But Jacob's real worry about the theater seems to have been the attraction of the music. He fretted to his congregation about "responses (or chorus, chants) which are not true; troublesome and confused sounds; melodies which attract children; ordered and cherished songs; skilful chants, lying canticles...Your ear is captivated by song."[18] The music of the theater told its stories in melodies and verses that lingered in the mind, hummed by children and adults alike. And thus Jacob fumed: We have better music here, in the church!

Rome in the East: The Transformation of an Empire, 246–305, esp. 304–5, New York: Routledge, 2001.

[16] "Jacob of Serugh's Homilies On the Spectacles of the Theatre", Hom. 5, trans. Cyril Moss, *Le Muséon* 48 (1935): 87–112, at pp. 108–9–3.

[17] Consider, for example, Jacob's homilies on Tamar (Gen. 38), and on Jephthah's Daughter (Jud. 11). See the discussion in Harvey, "Bride of Blood, Bride of Light".

[18] "On the Spectacles", Hom. 3, trans. Moss, *Le Muséon* 48 (1935): 105.

However, lest one think that only the life of the laity, with its burdens of family and work, income and the marketplace, provided temptation towards a certain devotional laxity, one should note that Jacob also preached against the complacency and temptations of the monastic life. In homilies clearly addressed to those in monastic vocations, Jacob intoned against boredom and lethargy. He sang the praises of poverty and fasting; called for focus, attention, and struggle. The Evil One was always near to distract the monk with anxious thoughts, desires, uncertainties. Like Lot and his wife, or the Wise and Foolish Virgins, the monk must choose to remain steadfast, or he could be defeated.[19]

However, overall it is not often that one can clearly delineate Jacob's homilies as addressing a specifically monastic audience, or a specifically civic one. In many of the homilies on biblical stories, the distinction is moot for his topic: the biblical story and its implications for the life of faith are applicable to all. On occasions such as the great feasts of the church, Jacob celebrates the presence of the entire ecclesial body in liturgical splendor: lay and religious, ordained and monastic, young and old, married and virgin. And in fact, it seems that in general, church congregations contained this spectrum even in ordinary services. Lay people often attended liturgies performed at monasteries, or at the columns of stylites, or at the cells of hermits. In turn, village, town, and city church services generally included monastics, even of rigorous solitary practice. Jacob himself indicates this in some of his homilies, but the situation is constantly attested in other historical sources of his time: in personal accounts, letters, church canons, chronicles, or saints' lives.[20]

One of the important characteristics of ancient Syriac Christianity (as now!) was the constant interaction of monastics, clergy, and laity, in the context of daily life, of devotional piety, and

---

[19] Memre 137 and 138, Bedjan 4: 818–36, 836–71.

[20] Harvey, S.A. "Praying Bodies, Bodies at Prayer: Ritual Relations in Early Syriac Christianity," in Allen, Pauline, Lawrence Cross, and Wendy Mayer, eds. *Prayer and Spirituality in the Early Church, vol. 4: the Spiritual Life*, 149–67, Sydney: St. Paul's Publications, 2006.

of liturgical service.[21] This intermingling of the different vocations of Christian life is crucial for understanding what Jacob means when he speaks of the Church in its gathered wholeness, or of worship properly performed: each person is a necessary part in order for the body to be whole. All are needed.

Jacob does not in fact understand the devotional obligations to be different for laity, monastics, or clergy in their essential discipline. Love of God, compassion for the poor, sick, and needy; service of the church; distance from worldly ambitions, material excess, greed, envy, or self-serving desires: such self-discipline in Jacob's view was required of every Christian, of every station in life, regardless of age or gender. Nonetheless, there is a kindness to the bridge Jacob sometimes draws in his homilies, to connect the two vocations of monastery and family. In his homily on the death of an ascetic woman (a Daughter of the Covenant, *bart qyomo*[22]), he praises her steadfast ascetic devotion and offers assurance that in death she entered the wedding feast with her beloved Heavenly Bridegroom, to whom she had betrothed herself in life.[23] The imagery is commonplace in Syriac tradition. Yet Jacob dwells upon the vocabulary of wedding banquets and marriage celebrations at great length here, using marital imagery to express monastic content. Elsewhere, in his homily on Jephthah's Daughter (Judges 11), he does the reverse: using monastic imagery to express marital grief. When he describes the Daughter's sojourn in the mountains with her friends to mourn her untimely death as a virgin, he uses the imagery of monastic renunciation to explore her tragic and untimely leave-taking of marriage and children. [24] In

---

[21] One thinks of St. Mark's Syriac Orthodox Cathedral in Teaneck, New Jersey, for example! Or in the Netherlands, at St. Ephrem's monastery in Glane; or most famously, in Tur 'Abdin at Mor Gabriel.

[22] Hom. 191, "On the death of a *bart qyomo*", Bedjan 5: 821–36. See also Kitchen, Robert. "The Pearl of Virginity: Death as the Reward of Asceticism in Memra 191 of Jacob of Serugh," *Hugoye* 7.2 (July 2004).

[23] Esp. at Bedjan 5: 824–6.

[24] Hom. 159, Bedjan 5: 306–30. An English translation see Harvey, Susan, and Ophir Münz-Manor, tr. and introd. *Jacob of Sarug's Homily on Jephthah's Daughter*, Texts from Christian Late Antiquity, 22, Gorgias Press,

both instances, one can well imagine that the homily was moving for all in the congregation, whether lay or monastic, whether parents or avowed ascetics.

2. THE SINGING CONGREGATION

But Jacob had more to say to and about his congregations than frustrated criticisms. His parishioners could and did conduct themselves in exemplary style on occasion, and never more so than when they came to church and took up their assigned task of singing hymns. Jacob's poetry shines incandescent when he calls his congregation to song. On the feast of the Nativity, for instance, he calls out, "Be awakened, O Church, with your beautiful chants,/ and offer to the Son gifts of praise on the day of his birth."[25] To Jacob, the singing of praise to God's glory is the real reason anything existed. In his homily on the first day of creation, Jacob describes how at the very moment "In the beginning", God created "heaven and earth and hidden hosts of the heights", establishing the ranks and orders of heavenly powers, seraphim, cherubim, angels and archangels, all with the purpose to sing.

> He established them, he ordered them, he set them in motion
>   to bless, to sanctify, to chant "hallelujah".
>   He filled their mouths with hallelujahs and shouts of joy
> so that they would always be singing glory naturally.[26]

Elsewhere, he speaks of nature and the whole of the created order as serving a continual liturgy of praise. Because creation sings "naturally", Jacob explains, as it was made, it sings by free will and not as a programmed machine. In this way, nature provided the model for human response to God: of our own free will, we should all be singing, all the time! For example, by their stately movement

---

2010. The passage discussed here is at lines 386–405. See also the discussion in Harvey, "Bride of Blood," 192.

[25] FH 1 (Nativity 1), p. 88–9, ll. 1037–8.

[26] "Jacob of Serugh, On the Establishment of Creation, Memra One, The First Day", trans. Robin Darling Young, in Wilson Trigg, J., ed. *Biblical Interpretation*, 184–202, at p. 191, MFC, 9, Wilmington, Del: Michael Glazier, 1988.

in time, nature's guards, Morning and Evening, instruct humankind in the wonders of God's works, and incite the singing of praise as appropriate response.

> Like deacons reverend, vigilant and undefiled,
> The morning and the evening establish the ranks [of the faithful] in [their] devotions.
> As marshallers of two mellifluous choirs,
> Each of them arouses daily cause for doxologies.
> The morning goes forth as ambassador for the day,
> and gets the world up to give glory at the arrival of light.
> The evening enters, whereat all creation becomes tumultuous,
> as it removes its hands from labor to chant hymns of praise.
> The morning and the evening endure unchanging, like luminous signs,
> and from them, the world learns to give glory.[27]

In his festal homilies, especially those for Nativity and Palm Sunday (the Sunday of Hosannas), Jacob delights to present the whole of God's creation, heaven and earth, natural, supernatural, and human, joined together in shared song of celebration. With lyrical grace, he intones these occasions as moments when the biblical past interlaces the liturgical present, and different biblical characters provide the types for how and why the different segments of the human church community can all participate in the joyful singing of God's glorious and saving works. Because a virgin conceived Christ, he exhorted, the choir of virgins can sing praise. Because Christ was born a baby to be cradled in the arms of his parents, babies in the arms of their parents are anointed and baptized in his name. Because Mary was chosen from human women to be his mother, mothers and husbands join in the festal songs. As Joseph, Mary, and the whole of creation sing because of the Christ child, so, too, all children, all pregnant mothers, all parents, all unmarried young virgins rejoice in song. Adam, Eve, and all the elderly rejoice; pastors and flocks, the Church, the

---

[27] "A Homily on the Giving of Praise for the Morning and Evening, by Mar Jacob, Bishop of Serugh", trans. HTM [Dana Miller], *The True Vine* 26 (1998): 59–64, at p. 62, ll. 69–78.

gatherings of peoples and congregations all sing together. And not least, Jacob chants at the Nativity feast, "Let the speaker and the hearers too rejoice in you, my Lord/ because by your Nativity you have gladdened them, to you be glory."[28]

Here, for example, is an abbreviated version of such a description from his homily for the Sunday of Hosannas:

> O my Lord, the mouths of human beings praise you with their
>   tongues,
> and the [mute] natures in their own ways sing your praise.
> … the whole of nature…
> …the heavens…
> and the earth…
> The redeemed gathering of the Church of the Peoples shouts
>   joyfully to you, my Lord,
>
> …
>
> Behold, the young people praise you with the branches of the
>   trees
> and the voice of praise of the aged is mixed with that of the
>   children.
> Behold, the shepherds and their flocks adore you.
>   (NB=bishops and churches)
>
> …
>
> Behold, the gatherings of the Peoples in all places bless you,
>
> …
>
> Behold, they call out to you, 'Holy, Holy, Holy,' in the
>   assemblies
>
> …
>
> Behold, all voices from all mouths are singing your praise
> with all tongues, since you have stirred them up for your
>   praise.
> Fiery Seraphs…
> Glorious Cherubs…
> Many thousands of heavenly beings sing your glory
> without ceasing from the praise of their sanctification.

---

[28] FH 3 (Nativity 3), pp. 112, 126–7, ll. 27–34, 342–70; cp. FH 4 (Nativity 4), p. 135–6, vv. 26–7.

...

All are giving thanks to you because by your coming
    everything is renewed;
you are blessed by all, to praise from all tongues.[29]

In such passages, Jacob identifies every member of the
gathered church as crucial to, and fully participant in, the activity of
liturgical celebration. Naming each group by gender, age, ethnicity
('the Peoples'/ the 'Nations'), social location, ecclesiastical rank,
Jacob effectively erases the lines between lay, monastic, and
ordained as worship celebrants. Or, more accurately, the laity
themselves become included as ritual participants whose role is as
necessary to the fulfillment of liturgical prescription as those of
ordained clergy and hierarchs. The Church becomes truly "a
priesthood of all believers" (1 Pet 2). This is nowhere proclaimed
with such visceral force as when Jacob portrays Christ the Good
Physician welcoming Eve, healed and restored, into his renewed
creation on the day of his Nativity. Because Christ healed and
welcomed Eve, 'the despised woman', Jacob insists, all women are
welcomed, even the most marginal. Jacob names them, one by one:
the barren woman, the humiliated woman, the sorrowful woman,
the lamenting woman, the enslaved woman, the possessed woman,
the imprisoned woman.[30] Jacob's insistence on the congregation's
all-inclusive constitution thus displays the congregation—female,
male, rich, poor, young, old— as a mirror for the wholeness of
humanity redeemed. In this role—themselves as living icons of
salvific grace—the congregation are rendered not only the audience
who receive Jacob's preaching, but his co-workers in the
declaration of divine mercy. From the sheer exuberance of Jacob's
praise for his congregation's singing during festal liturgies, we can
be sure that sometimes they did in fact behave as he would wish.

---

[29] FH 10 (Sunday of Hosannas), pp. 259–60, ll. 275–304.
[30] FH 1 (Nativity 1), pp. 88–9, ll. 1039–56.

3. ORDINARY GRACE

Jacob spent most of his career traveling throughout the district of Serugh preaching at vigils, serving daily offices and celebrating liturgies. In his homilies we glimpse his congregation amidst its every-day world; for in his exasperated criticism and his delighted praise, Jacob also shows us who they were by the lives they lived. The reverse to his complaints of their behavior looked like this: his parishioners were hardworking, beleaguered, and harried men and women struggling to provide for their families, seeking respite from the pressures of their burdens. They were newly weds longing for children, frightened of the dangers even as they craved the wonders of new life. They were the widowed and bereaved, worn, exhausted, and lonely. They were monks and nuns who struggled in all sincerity to work with unflagging commitment at the daily grind of self-sufficiency, while earnestly striving for illumination of the heart. They were ordinary villagers and townspeople who at the same time served their churches faithfully as deacons and deaconesses, chanters and readers, choir members, pastors, and teachers. And now and then, they all managed to sing together, in tune, in harmony, at the right time, and in the right place.

Jacob's work was not the glamorous thrill of establishing something new; nor the heady exultation of seeing a gamble succeed, triumphant and victorious. His was the work of keeping things going; not in the exciting rush of cosmopolitan cities, with their sophistication and turbulence, but rather in the often sleepy hinterland of the late antique eastern Mediterranean. It is the very ordinariness of Jacob's work, preaching and teaching year in and year out throughout a sprawling countryside, that I often think of when I read his homilies. There is one passage to which I often return.

In one of his homilies on the Nativity, Jacob describes the Virgin Mary after she has made her decision to accept God's call and receive the conception of his divine Son. He pauses to imagine the interlude after her encounter with the archangel Gabriel and before her reception of the Holy Spirit, the moment in between these two miraculous encounters. In that moment, Jacob imagines Mary preparing herself for what will happen next. She is about to receive her Lord as a guest in her own body; she must present herself appropriately. So Jacob imagines Mary as a housekeeper preparing for royalty to visit. She cleans, dusts, tidies up and repairs the house of her soul, sweeping away any unworthy thoughts, casting out any worthless sentiments, polishing up the shine of her virtues. She mends the damaged or worn parts, sets anything messy in order. She freshens, replenishes, and renews with sweet thoughts, good intentions, and reverence. She adorns and embellishes with piety, virtues, and prayer. As she works, she sings hymns of thanksgiving. When all is radiant and beautiful, she opens the door and invites her Lord to enter.[31]

In this poignant depiction, Jacob presents the earnest effort of the village housewife. But here, too, was the quiet labor of the priest preparing his church and its sanctuary in the interlude before the people came for the service to begin—a service that would bring divine presence into their lives. I think, in fact, that here Jacob presents himself, attending to the work of preparing a place worthy for God's arrival. That place was not only in the church buildings (large or small) in which he served liturgy. It was also in the hearts of his congregation, the ordinary people to whom he preached.

---

[31] FH 1 (Nativity 1), pp. 59–60, 387–418. For discussion of this extraordinary passage, see Harvey, S.A. "Interior Decorating: Jacob of Serugh on Mary's Preparation for the Incarnation," *Studia Patristica* 41, ed. F. Young, M. Edwards and P. Parvis, 23–8, Leuven: Peeters, 2006.